ABOUT MAGIC READERS

ABDO continues its commitment to quality books with the nonfiction Magic Readers series. This series includes three levels of books to help students progress to being independent readers while learning factual information. Different levels are intended to reflect the stages of reading in the early grades, helping to select the best level for each individual student.

level 1

Level 1: Books with short sentences and familiar words or patterns to share with children who are beginning to understand how letters and sounds go together.

level 2

Level 2: Books with longer words and sentences and more complex language patterns with less repetition for progressing readers who are practicing common words and letter sounds.

level 3

Level 3: Books with more developed language and vocabulary for transitional readers who are using strategies to figure out unknown words and are ready to learn information more independently.

These nonfiction readers are aligned with the Common Core State Standards progression of literacy, following the sequence of skills and increasing the difficulty of language while engaging the curious minds of young children. These books also reflect the increasing importance of reading informational material in the early grades. They encourage children to read for fun and to learn!

Hannah E. Tolles, MA Reading Specialist

www.abdopublishing.com

Published by Magic Wagon, a division of ABDO, PO Box 398166, Minneapolis, Minnesota 55439. Copyright © 2015 by Abdo Consulting Group, Inc. International copyrights reserved in all countries. No part of this book may be reproduced in any form without written permission from the publisher. Magic Readers™ is a trademark and logo of Magic Wagon.

Printed in the United States of America, North Mankato, Minnesota.
062014
092014

Cover Photo: Thinkstock
Interior Photos: Getty Images, iStockphoto, Science Source, Shutterstock, Thinkstock

Written and edited by Rochelle Baltzer, Heidi M. D. Elston, Megan M. Gunderson, and Bridget O'Brien
Illustrated by Candice Keimig
Designed by Candice Keimig and Jillian O'Brien

Library of Congress Cataloging-in-Publication Data

Elston, Heidi M. D., 1979- author.
 Snakes in the desert / Heidi M.D. Elston [and three others] ; designed and illustrated by Candice Keimig.
    pages cm. -- (Magic readers. Level 3)
 Audience: Ages 5-8.
 ISBN 978-1-62402-071-1
1. Rattlesnakes--Juvenile literature. 2. Rattlesnakes--Habitat--Juvenile literature. I. Keimig, Candice, illustrator. II. Title.
 QL666.O69E475 2015
 597.96'38--dc23
             2014013777

Snakes
in the Desert

By Heidi M. D. Elston
Illustrated photos by Candice Keimig

Magic Readers

An Imprint of Magic Wagon
www.abdopublishing.com

Rattlesnakes live from southern Canada to Argentina.

Many live in the desert. Some
also live in swamps or meadows.

There are 30 kinds of rattlesnakes.

Western
Diamondback

Timber

Banded
Rock

Eastern
Diamondback

Some are just 1 foot long. Others can grow to 8 feet!

Rattlesnakes come in many different colors and patterns.

This is a red diamondback.
It is brick red with a diamond
pattern.

This is a Southwestern speckled rattlesnake. It is gray with stripes.

This pattern helps it hide in the rocks.

This is an eastern diamondback
rattlesnake.

Its name tells where it lives.
It lives in the southeastern
United States.

A snake uses its senses to stay safe from predators.

If a snake senses danger, it may stay still or hide.

A rattlesnake has a rattle on the end of its tail.

When danger is near, it rattles its tail. It also hisses and puffs up its body.

The snake's rattle is a warning.
Stay away!

The snake may bite quickly. The bite is painful.

A snake bites with its two long fangs.

A poison called venom comes out
of the fangs. This can be deadly.

Rattlesnakes live in many states.

Hikers may see rattlesnakes. So, people are careful where they step.

Rattlesnakes are shy. They want to be left alone.

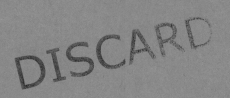

DIOGENES

M. D. Usher • Pictures by **Michael Chesworth**

Farrar, Straus and Giroux
New York

To street dogs everywhere, and especially those of modern Athens —M.D.U.

For Mr. Frigidus —M.C.

*Heaven goes by favor. If it went by merit, you would stay out
and your dog would go in. —Mark Twain*

I sound my barbaric yawp over the roofs of the world. —Walt Whitman

*I am called a dog because I wag my tail for those who give, I bark at those who don't,
and I bare my teeth at rogues. —Diogenes*

Text copyright © 2009 by M. D. Usher
Pictures copyright © 2009 by Michael Chesworth
All rights reserved
Distributed in Canada by Douglas & McIntyre Ltd.
Printed and bound in the United States of America by Worzalla
Designed by Jay Colvin
First edition, 2009
10 9 8 7 6 5 4 3 2 1

www.fsgkidsbooks.com

Library of Congress Cataloging-in-Publication Data
Usher, Mark David, date.
    Diogenes / M.D. Usher ; pictures by Michael Chesworth.— 1st ed.
        p. cm.
    Summary: Not content to sit, stay, roll over, or play fetch, a dog in ancient
Greece decides to live a master-free life, like the mouse. End notes discuss the
life and teachings of the Greek philosopher Diogenes.
    ISBN-13: 978-0-374-31785-0
    ISBN-10: 0-374-31785-2
    [1. Dogs—Fiction.   2. Conduct of life—Fiction.   3. Self-actualization
(Psychology)—Fiction.   4. Diogenes, d. ca. 323 B.C.—Fiction.   5. Greece—
History—To 146 B.C.—Fiction.]   I. Chesworth, Michael, ill.   II. Title.
PZ7.U6955 Di 2009
[E]—dc22
                                                    2007037703

All translations from the Greek are the author's.

This is the story of a remarkable dog who lived a long time ago in ancient Greece.
His name was Diogenes.

Most dogs in this world are content with their doggy lives.

They sit, stay, roll over, fetch, play dead—you know, the usual tricks dogs do for a treat, or to win a spot at the foot of their master's bed.

Diogenes was different. He wanted to be his own master.

One day, while his friends were up to their usual tricks,
Diogenes noticed a mouse.

The mouse did not sit, stay, roll over, fetch, or play dead. Nor
did she worry about what kind of food she would eat or where
she would sleep.

She just scurried about, unafraid of the dark—unbothered, in fact, by anything at all.

"Woof," said Diogenes softly. "I want to be like this mouse."

Diogenes knew that in order to live like the mouse, he needed to learn some new tricks. So he did a very brave and unusual thing: He buried his collar and leash, left his cozy doghouse, and ran off to the city with his dog dish, a walking stick, and nothing more.

Diogenes felt unbelievably free—as if a great burden had been lifted from his back.

"I like being my own master," he thought.

The greatest city in Greece in those days was Athens,
so that's where Diogenes went. Athens was magnificent.
It teemed with temples, gardens, and luxurious art.

But although the people of Athens were rich, they did not seem happy. They looked comfortable, but not content.

"Now *this* looks like a good place to try some new tricks!" Diogenes thought to himself.

Diogenes' first trick was to need as little as possible—and to want even less than that.

When he was hungry, he begged for his food. When he was sleepy, he just curled up in an old pot.

He learned other tricks, too: To get used to the heat of summer, he'd roll around in hot sand. To get better at enduring winter's cold, he'd hug things covered in snow.

Sometimes he even begged from statues.
"Why in the world are you doing that?" someone asked him.
"To get good at being refused," he said with a smile.
He *really* liked being his own master.

Diogenes was determined to live as simply as he could. One day, he saw a young boy use his cupped hand to drink water.

"Woof!" said Diogenes. "Now *that's* a good trick!" And he threw even his dog dish away.

The Athenians wondered where this odd dog had come from. "Are you from Corinth? Sparta? Argos? Thebes?" they asked. "None of these," said Diogenes proudly. "The whole world is my home!"

Diogenes was happy with his simple life. He spent his mornings in the park and lounged about all afternoon in the cool porches and temples of Athens. People asked him if he missed having his own house and garden.

"Why should I?" he replied, waving his paw at the great buildings and beauty around him. "I live like a king!"

People thought Diogenes was strange. Sometimes he would walk through town in broad daylight carrying a lantern.

"What in the world are you doing with that lantern?" people would ask.

"Looking for a good man," he would reply with a bark. (Good people, you know, are often so hard to find you need a light to see them, even in the sunshine.)

Diogenes soon became the most famous dog in Greece. People traveled from all over to see his latest trick.

One morning, as he was sunning himself in front of his pot, the ruler of the world, Alexander the Great, stopped by for a visit.

Alexander was a king. He was powerful and rich and thought a lot of himself.

"Ask for whatever you want," said Alexander, puffing out his chest with pride, "and you shall have it!"

But Diogenes was quite content with what he had. He was his own master.

Diogenes yawned, then opened one eye and made his request: "Would you please step aside? You're blocking my sun."

The king was taken aback. "Hmmm," he said, scratching his head. "If I weren't Alexander, I think I would want to be Diogenes."

"Yes, this is a good life," thought Diogenes.

Then one day, when Diogenes was walking through the countryside to look for good men there . . .

a dogcatcher snatched him up and took him off to the pound.

The pound was dark, dingy, and damp. Diogenes thought of the mouse. "I'm still my own master," he said with a twinkle in his eye.

Not long after, a rich merchant happened to walk past the pound. He wore golden slippers and a silk gown, and you could tell he was very fond of his money.

Diogenes pointed at the man and yapped, "Hey, give me to him! He needs to learn a trick or two!"

The man, who in his heart was a good man, stopped to have a look at Diogenes. "What tricks can you do?" he asked.

"I know how to be my own master," Diogenes said, wagging his tail. "And I can teach you to be your own master, too."

The man was intrigued.

"This must be an exceptionally smart dog," he said to himself.
So he brought Diogenes home to take care of his children.

The children loved Diogenes, and he loved them, too.
Together they romped and roamed. And—of course—
Diogenes taught the whole family every trick he knew.

People say it's a dog's life. And, you know, if a dog's his own master . . . they're absolutely right.

AFTERWORD

This story is completely true. Well, almost. The real Diogenes was, you may have guessed, not an actual dog, but a man who founded the so-called Cynic school of philosophy. But even here there's an element of truth, for the word *cynic* means "dog-like" in ancient Greek. Diogenes' contemporaries called him a Cynic because, like a dog, he did all his private business out in the open and wasn't embarrassed about it in the least. The nickname was meant as an insult, but Diogenes eagerly adopted it as a badge of honor and took upon himself the role of "watchdog" to those around him, warning them of life's moral pitfalls—lethargy, luxury, ambition, stupidity, greed.

Diogenes was born around 412 B.C. in a town called Sinope (si-NOH-pee) on the Black Sea, where as a boy he himself lived a life of luxury and ease. His father, Hicesias (hi-KEE-zee-yus), was a banker there, but when his father was accused of tampering with the city's coinage, Diogenes was forced to move out of town. It was a decisive moment in his life. From that point on—for reasons that aren't perfectly clear to us now, though it does seem to have had something to do with his observation of a mouse—Diogenes dedicated himself to a life of voluntary poverty and of questioning commonly held practices and beliefs. He moved to Athens, where he became a student of Antisthenes (an-TISS-the-neez), one of Socrates' followers, and later attracted disciples of his own.

Diogenes, undated Roman copy of an undated Greek original statuette. Villa Albani, Rome. Photograph used with permission of Alinari Archives, Florence

Diogenes was famous for his witty remarks and the many stunts he performed in order to illustrate a philosophical point. These are the "tricks" recounted in the story. He felt that people were far too concerned with money, power, and prestige, and that the false values of civilized society were responsible for these delusions. Instead, Diogenes argued, people should look to nature for their example of how to live. However, because most of us have become too "civilized" and spoiled to live fully according to nature, we need some practice or

Relief with Diogenes and Alexander the Great,
100 B.C.–A.D. 100. Villa Albani, Rome.
Photograph used with permission of Alinari
Archives, Florence

training. The Cynics called this *askesis*
(AH-skay-siss)—a word they borrowed from
the world of Greek athletics (and whence our
word "ascetic"). And so they lived outdoors,
ate whatever food came their way, hugged cold
statues, and rolled around in hot sand.

Diogenes also believed strongly in free
speech—*parrhesia* (pah-ray-SEE-uh) in
Greek—which he considered the finest thing
in the world. By "free speech" he meant the
courage and capacity to say whatever one
thinks is right, in whatever way might be most
effective, to whoever needs to hear it, no
matter what the consequences. The ultimate goal of a Cynic's life, however, was to
achieve *autarkeia* (ow-TAR-kay-uh), or "self-sufficiency," which Diogenes and his
followers regarded as a kind of physical, intellectual, and moral independence
from the ill-considered views and lifestyles of society at large. *Autarkeia*, in short,
is the art of being one's own master.

For all his poverty and freethinking, Diogenes really did live happily ever
after—and to a ripe old age—as a tutor in the household of a rich man called
Xeniades (ze-NYE-uh-deez) from Corinth. He was never sent to the pound
(obviously) but, rather, captured by pirates and sold to Xeniades as a slave to be
the tutor of his children. Xeniades' children fell in love with their new teacher, and
it wasn't long before they themselves started to copy Diogenes' lifestyle. In fact,
they became Cynic philosophers when they grew up!

When Diogenes died, the city of Corinth erected a marble statue of a dog over
his grave and dedicated a bronze monument with these words inscribed:

Diogenes, though bronze grows gray with time,
Your glory is forever in its prime.
You showed the smoothest road in life's ascent
Is to be with our own selves content.